THE CIVIL WAR
WEAPONS

BY JIM OLLHOFF

VISIT US AT
WWW.ABDOPUBLISHING.COM

Published by ABDO Publishing Company, PO Box 398166, Minneapolis, MN 55439.
Copyright ©2012 by Abdo Consulting Group, Inc. International copyrights reserved in all
countries. No part of this book may be reproduced in any form without written permission from
the publisher. ABDO & Daughters™ is a trademark and logo of ABDO Publishing Company.

Printed in the United States of America, North Mankato, Minnesota.
122011
012012

 PRINTED ON RECYCLED PAPER

Editor: John Hamilton
Graphic Design: Sue Hamilton
Cover Design: Neil Klinepier
Cover Photo: John Hamilton
Interior Photos and Illustrations: AP-pgs 17 (inset) & 24-25; Corbis-pgs 10 & 23 (inset);
Getty-pgs 18-19 & 26-27; Granger Collection-pgs 22-23; John Hamilton-pgs 4-5, 6 (inset),
7, 8 (inset), 9 & 14-15; Library of Congress-pgs 1, 3, 11, 12-13, 16-17, 20-21, 28 (inset) & 29;
Mike Cumpston-pg 10 (inset); National Archives-pgs 6, 8 & 28; Signal Corps Association-pg 18;
U.S. Navy-pg 25 (inset).

ABDO Booklinks

To learn more about the Civil War, visit ABDO Publishing Company online. Web sites about
the Civil War are featured on our Book Links pages. These links are routinely monitored and
updated to provide the most current information available. Web site: www.abdopublishing.com

Library of Congress Cataloging-in-Publication Data

Ollhoff, Jim, 1959-
  The Civil War : weapons / Jim Ollhoff.
    p. cm. -- (The Civil War)
  Includes index.
  ISBN 978-1-61783-278-9
  1. United States--History--Civil War, 1861-1865--Equipment and supplies--Juvenile literature.
2. United States. Army--Weapons systems--History--19th century--Juvenile literature. 3.
Confederate States of America. Army--Weapons systems--Juvenile literature. 4. United States--
History--Civil War, 1861-1865--Technology--Juvenile literature. 5. Military weapons--United
States--History--19th century--Juvenile literature. I. Title. II. Title: Weapons.
  E491.O45 2012
  973.7'8--dc23
                                 2011039981

CONTENTS

Union troops stand with the "Dictator," a cannon that shot 200-pound (91-kg) shells.

WEAPONS OF THE CIVIL WAR

The American Civil War was a turning point in the history of warfare. In battles throughout the 1700s and early 1800s, armies fought by lining up facing each other and shooting their muskets. The firearms in those days were so inaccurate that soldiers had to be at very close range in order to have a good chance of hitting the enemy. After they got off a volley of musket fire, the two sides would charge each other. Bayonets, the knives attached to the ends of firearms, did almost as much damage as musket balls in actual warfare.

Generals of the 19th century studied the strategy of Napoleon Bonaparte (1769–1821), the great French military leader. Napoleon led his armies across Europe, and was frighteningly efficient in battle. Many paintings of Napoleon show him with one hand tucked inside his coat. Some Civil War generals had photographs taken with their hand in their coat, because they wanted to be like Napoleon.

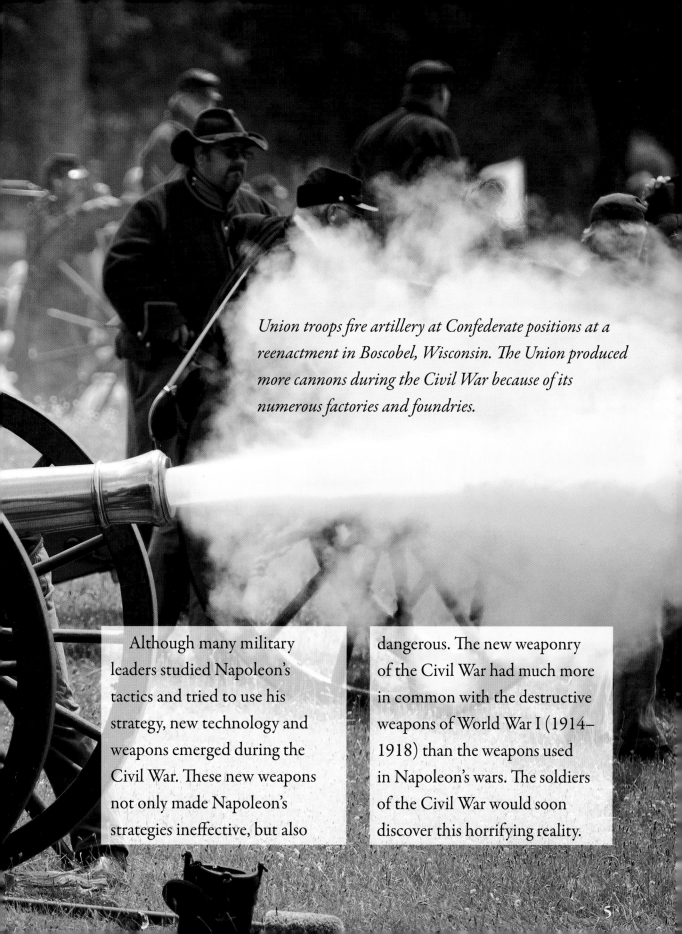

Union troops fire artillery at Confederate positions at a reenactment in Boscobel, Wisconsin. The Union produced more cannons during the Civil War because of its numerous factories and foundries.

Although many military leaders studied Napoleon's tactics and tried to use his strategy, new technology and weapons emerged during the Civil War. These new weapons not only made Napoleon's strategies ineffective, but also dangerous. The new weaponry of the Civil War had much more in common with the destructive weapons of World War I (1914–1918) than the weapons used in Napoleon's wars. The soldiers of the Civil War would soon discover this horrifying reality.

SWORDS AND BLADES

Before the Civil War, knives, swords, and bayonets were important weapons for infantry soldiers. Before the Civil War, soldiers stood in a line and shot their firearms at the enemy, usually with smoothbore weapons such as muskets. Since these firearms were so inaccurate, relatively few soldiers were actually hit by the bullets.

With their ammunition spent, the soldiers then charged toward the enemy with bladed weapons. Soldiers on horseback often used sabers, which had curved sword blades for slashing. In the years before the Civil War, bladed weapons caused most battlefield wounds.

The American Civil War changed all that. New technology was used to manufacture bullets and rifles that were more accurate. Battlefields became a sea of blood and wounded men, all hit by bullets or artillery fire at long range. Bladed weapons were simply obsolete.

Reenactors with bayonets.

Reenactors demonstrate saber combat on horseback.

Of the thousands of injured Civil War soldiers, only about 900 were wounded by knives or swords. Most of those wounds came from disagreements and fights between people in camp, rather than on the battlefield.

Mostly, swords were given only to officers. Some officers liked to carry them because it made them feel important. Other officers stopped carrying swords because the weapons were clumsy and heavy.

FIREARMS

Before the Civil War, battles were fought with flintlock smoothbore muskets. The inside of the barrel was smooth. Gunpowder was first poured into the barrel. The bullet, usually a lead ball, was then inserted into the barrel, along with a small piece of paper or cloth (wadding) to keep the ball from falling out. When the soldier pulled the trigger, a hammer with a flint tip struck a steel plate, causing a spark. This spark ignited the gunpowder. The resulting explosion forced the lead ball out of the barrel.

A smoothbore flintlock musket.

Smoothbore muskets were not very accurate. They had an effective range of about 70-100 yards (64-91 m) or less. Muskets had to be reloaded after each shot. Most soldiers could fire them only 2-3 times per minute.

When the Civil War began, the Confederacy didn't have many modern gun-making facilities. Until more factories got up and running around mid-1862, most Confederate soldiers used old smoothbore muskets. Many brought their own weapons from home.

A better firearm was called a rifled musket. Most Union soldiers used this weapon. The inside of the barrel was grooved, not smooth. This caused bullets to spin as they came out of the barrel. Because of this spin, bullets could travel farther, and were more accurate.

Civil War reenactors armed with muskets. The average age of a Civil War soldier was 25, but boys as young as 12 were often sent into battle. Some estimate that 100,000 Union soldiers were less than 15 years old. Many lied about their age.

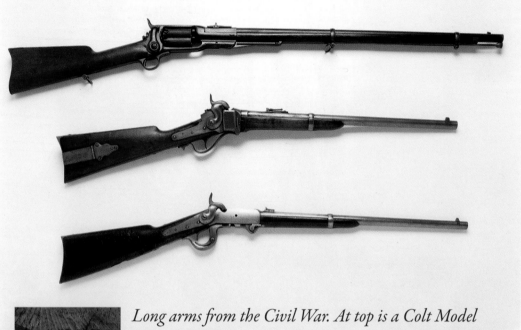

Long arms from the Civil War. At top is a Colt Model 1853 Revolving Rifle used by sharpshooters. In the middle is a Sharps carbine, often used by Union cavalry troops. Below is a Burnside carbine, which was invented by Union General Ambrose Burnside.

Minie balls

Another deadly new innovation was a bullet called a minie ball. No longer did rifles fire a round lead ball. The minie ball was a cone-shaped bullet. It was accurate at a distance up to 250 yards (229 m). Soldiers could fire rifled muskets about three times per a minute.

Cavalrymen—those on horses—liked using breech-loading carbines. The breech is where the barrel connects to the firing mechanism. On breech-loading carbines, soldiers loaded the bullets at the breech. This made the weapon smaller and easier to fire, which was especially important while riding a horse.

Another weapon used by cavalrymen was the revolver handgun. It had a rotating cylinder. It was fast and easy to shoot, and was used when cavalrymen rushed enemy lines.

Corporal Elias Warner of Company K, 3rd New York Cavalry Regiment, with an 1852 Slant Breech Sharps carbine and cavalry saber.

LOADING AND FIRING RIFLES

The process of loading and firing a rifle required several steps. The soldier stood with his rifle in front of him. He took out his cartridge, a paper envelope filled with gunpowder and the bullet. He tore the cartridge open with his teeth, and poured the powder down the barrel. Then he dropped the lead ball or minie ball down the barrel, followed by the paper. He pushed it all down with a thin piece of metal called a ramrod. Then he pulled the hammer back and attached a percussion cap, which when struck would create a small explosion and ignite the main powder inside the gun barrel. Finally, the soldier pointed the rifle at the enemy and pulled the trigger.

The steps of loading and firing a rifle took a long time, and in the chaos of battle, generals were afraid that soldiers would lose their place. So, the men stood in a line, and officers called out each step, waiting for all the men to finish before calling out the next step. They would all shoot at the same time, and then start the process all over again.

Five Union soldiers of the 6th Regiment Massachusetts Volunteer Militia, outfitted with Enfield muskets.

DEADLY TACTICS

Throughout the 1700s and up until the 1830s, armies would line up and shoot off a volley of gunfire, then charge at each other with their bayonets. The bayonet did more damage than the rifles ever did. Generals in the Civil War were very familiar with that old strategy, and they insisted that their soldiers follow the same routine.

Union reenactors line up in an open field to attack Confederate forces.

However, there was one big problem. Weapons technology had changed. Significant improvements had been made by weapons developers. Rifles and cannons were much more accurate and deadly, and they were able to load faster. Not realizing how much technology had changed the weapons of war, Civil War generals used old strategy with new weapons, with horrifying results. Hundreds of troops would charge a position, only to be mowed down by accurate rifles and deadly cannons. The Civil War became a terrible bloodbath.

Later in the war, some generals began to change their strategy. Soldiers dug into defensive trenches. They used small, fast groups on horseback. They also conducted surprise attacks. But one of the reasons for the terrible numbers of losses in the Civil War was simply that, for the most part, war strategy did not catch up with the new technology.

BOMBS, LAND MINES, AND TORPEDOES

Land mines were bombs that sat on the ground and exploded when a person or vehicle put weight on them. Confederate General Gabriel Rains tried a number of these land mines, without much success at first. But, by 1863, he was planting them in many places, intending to slow down Union troops. In fact, almost 100 years later, in 1960, several of Rains's land mines were discovered. The powder was still active and the mines were still dangerous.

More common in the Civil War were naval mines, bombs that were tethered to the bottom of a river or harbor. When a ship's hull struck a mine, it exploded. During the Civil War, these were called torpedoes.

When Union ships sailed into Southern ports, torpedoes were a hazard. Since the Confederacy had few warships, torpedoes were a cheap and effective way to keep Union ships from getting too close or sailing up rivers. By the end of the war, torpedoes had sunk 29 ships.

Above: A Confederate arsenal on display in Charleston, South Carolina.

Right: Confederate barrel bombs were used to blow up Union ships in Southern waters.

REPEATING RIFLES AND THE GATLING GUN

A cross-section of a Spencer repeating rifle.

Inventors on both sides of the Civil War tried hard to make better firearms. One of the things they built was a firearm that didn't need to be loaded with powder and a bullet each time a soldier wanted to shoot. These weapons were called repeating rifles. One of these was the Spencer repeating rifle. Developed by Christopher Spencer in 1860, it could shoot up to 20 times per minute. Traditional rifled muskets could only shoot two to three times per minute. The Union army decided against the Spencer rifle at first. It required special bullets, and the army was unsure if it could supply enough ammunition for soldiers all over the country. The ammunition also produced a thick cloud of smoke. But in 1863, President Abraham Lincoln saw the rifle in action and ordered it into production.

Another invention was the Gatling gun. It was created by Richard Gatling in 1861. The Gatling gun was the earliest machine gun. It had six rifle barrels that rotated with a hand crank. It could fire 200 times per minute.

However, it often overheated, jammed frequently, and wasn't very accurate. It saw only limited use in the Civil War. In the years ahead, improvements in the Gatling gun would make it a feared weapon on the battlefield.

A Gatling gun at an arsenal in Washington, D.C., May 26, 1866.

ARTILLERY

Cannons, or artillery, were the big weapons of the Civil War. For the first part of the war, the Union had more artillery than the Confederacy, since most of the artillery factories were located in the Northern states.

Artillery guns were named after the kind of ammunition they used, such as "12-pound" (5.4 kg) or "24-pound" (10.9 kg) artillery. They were also labeled like rifle barrels, whether they were smooth on the inside (smoothbore) or grooved (rifled).

The most common Union artillery was the 12-pound (5.4 kg) smoothbore model 1857 Napoleon cannon. It could hit a target at a range up to 1,700 yards (1,554 m), but it was most effective with much closer targets, at about 250 yards (229 m).

The most common artillery projectile was called a canister. It was a can or wrapping of iron balls, which exploded above the charging enemy. After the canister exploded, the iron balls scattered at high velocity, causing massive damage to the enemy. With soldiers approaching in open fields with no cover or helmets, it was a devastating weapon, causing terrible wounds and death.

Transporting Civil War artillery was often a difficult and time-consuming process. A battery was usually made up of four to six cannons. It sometimes took up to 100 horses to move the artillery, equipment, and soldiers from place to place.

Union soldiers with cannons in an artillery bunker at Fort Richardson, Arlington, Virginia, in the 1860s.

IRONCLAD SHIPS

One of the first strategies of the Union was to create a naval blockade of Confederate seaports. This prevented the Confederacy from getting supplies from port to port. It also prevented the South from selling cotton to England.

In response to this blockade, the Confederacy took a captured Union vessel, the USS *Merrimack*, and attached iron plates to the hull. This protected it from Union cannon fire. They re-named the ship the CSS *Virginia*. The iron-hulled ship was finished on March 8, 1862. It immediately steamed out into the waters of Virginia and destroyed one Union ship, and forced two more to surrender. Cannonballs simply bounced off the sloped iron plates of the *Virginia*.

But the Union had also been working on an ironclad ship. Its name was the USS *Monitor*. The *Monitor* had a rotating turret on top, so it could fire its gun no matter which way the ship was facing. On March 9, the next morning, the *Monitor* sailed into the area. A four-hour battle took place between the two ironclads. The battle was a draw. Both damaged ships retreated. Even though the battle was a draw, it meant the end of wooden naval ships forever. Many more ironclads were built by both sides and used in battle during the Civil War.

Officers look at cannonball dents in the Monitor's *rotating turret.*

In 1862, the Union's *Monitor* (below left) and the Confederacy's *Virginia* (below right with flag) became the first ironclads to battle each other. Cannonball hits that would have sunk wooden ships caused only minor damage to the iron-plated ships.

SUBMARINES

Submarines of all shapes and sizes had been designed and built since the 1600s. However, the Confederate submarine *H. L. Hunley* was the first submarine to sink a warship. The *Hunley* was named after Horace Lawson Hunley, one of the people who funded it. Launched in July 1863, the 40-foot (12-m) long craft was designed to combat Union ships that were blockading Confederate ports.

With an eight-man Confederate crew, the *Hunley* was the first submarine to sink an enemy ship on February 17, 1864.

A cutaway illustration of the Hunley.

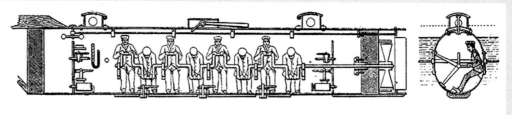

Eight crewmen hand-cranked its propeller. An officer steered the submarine and gave orders. A long pole in the front had a torpedo attached, which would be rammed into an enemy warship.

In practice, the *Hunley* had already sunk twice, killing its crews. But the idea of sneaking underwater to destroy a blockade was just too good to give up. The submarine was repaired and put back into service. On February 17, 1864, the *Hunley* attacked the USS *Housatonic* outside the harbor of Charleston, South Carolina. The *Housatonic* exploded and sank. The *Hunley* pulled away, but never returned to port. It was lost at sea, its sinking a mystery.

The wreck of the *Hunley* was discovered in 1995, about 100 yards (91 m) from the wreck of the *Housatonic*. The wreck of the *Hunley* was raised August 8, 2000, and taken to a facility in Charleston, South Carolina, where archaeologists could study it. The remains of the crew were still in the *Hunley*. They were removed, identified, and then given a military burial.

Study of the *Hunley* has not given a positive answer about why it sank. Archeologists did discover that the crew had not turned on a water pump. This might have affected oxygen levels in the submarine. So it may be that the crew misjudged the amount of oxygen they had. It's also possible the *Hunley* was damaged by the torpedo blast, or was accidentally rammed by another Union warship. The *Hunley* and her brave crew forever changed naval battles.

A view inside the *Hunley* after careful cleaning and restoration by archaeologists. The bodies of all eight crew members were found inside, as well as many Civil War-era artifacts.

OTHER NEW TECHNOLOGY

Many military innovations were used in the Civil War. One of the most important was the use of railroads. For the first time, railroads transported troops and supplies to the battlefield. When one side attacked, the other side often needed to simply hold out until trains could rush in fresh reinforcements. Railroads also became prime targets for attacks.

Soldiers stand guard atop a train as supplies are loaded.

For the first time in warfare, telegraphs were used to transmit information. Generals could keep up on what was happening in different battles. Presidents could stay current on the war. Telegrams became important tools to inform leaders so that they could direct the battles.

A man cuts a telegraph wire to stop enemy battle information from going out.

Another new tool used in the Civil War were giant hot air balloons, floating high above the battlefield. Balloons carried observers who watched enemy troop movements.

Sometimes they trailed a telegraph line from the balloon to the ground, so that generals could get immediate information on enemy troop numbers and movements.

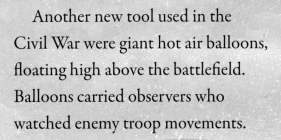

The *Intrepid* was one of seven balloons used by the Union army to spy on Confederate troops from high in the air. Each balloon had enough cable to climb 5,000 feet (1,524 m). Enemy numbers and locations were telegraphed to Union commanders on the ground.

GLOSSARY

ARSENAL

A fort where weapons and ammunition are stored.

ARTILLERY

Large weapons of war, such as cannons, used by military forces on land.

BATTERY

A group of similarly-sized heavy weapons used by a military force as a single fighting entity. During the Civil War, a battery was usually made up of four to six cannons.

BLOCKADE

The Union's plan to block ships from leaving Southern ports, and prevent ships from entering Southern ports.

CIVIL WAR

A war where two parts of the same nation fight against each other. The American Civil War was fought between Northern and Southern states from 1861–1865. The Southern states were for slavery. They wanted to start their own country. Northern states fought against slavery and a division of the country.

CONFEDERACY

The Southern states of Alabama, Arkansas, Florida, Georgia, Louisiana, Mississippi, North Carolina, South Carolina, Tennessee, Texas, and

Virginia. These states wanted to keep slavery legal. They broke away from the United States during the Civil War and formed their own country known as the Confederate States of America, or simply the Confederacy. The Confederacy ended in 1865 when the war ended and the 11 Confederate states rejoined the United States.

IRONCLADS

Steamships that had been outfitted with iron plates on the hull, so that cannonballs would bounce off the sides.

RIFLED BARREL

Rifled barrels have spiral grooves cut on the inside of the barrel—the part that the bullet travels down. Rifling greatly increases the accuracy of a weapon.

SMOOTHBORE BARREL

Smoothbore weapons are constructed with barrels—the part the bullet travels down—that are smooth. When the gun is fired, the ammunition bounces from side to side until it emerges from the barrel. The bullet's bouncing motion greatly decreases the weapon's accuracy.

TORPEDOES

Stationary mines tethered to the bottom of a harbor, which would blow up when touched by a ship.

UNION

The Northern states united against the Confederacy. "Union" also refers to all of the states of the United States. President Lincoln wanted to preserve the Union, keeping the Northern and Southern states together.

INDEX